W9-ABB-881

Written by Michael Smith

Illustrated by Octavio Oliva

East West Discovery Press

Manhattan Beach, California

The sky is high,

the trees are low.

The trees are high,

the grass is low.

The grass is high,

the ants are low.

What is high,

and what is low?

Planes go fast,

and cars go slow.

Cars go fast,
and kids go slow.

Kids go fast,
and snails go slow.
And snails go fast,
and trees grow slow.

Trees grow slow,

don’t you know?

Trees grow high,
oh my, oh my.

What is high, and what is low?

Who is fast, and who is slow?

Something is always higher
and something is always lower,
or faster, or slower,
or hotter, or colder.

And those are the facts.

As you can see,

it is all about...

"What is relativity?"

you may ask.

Finding out should be your task.

There is no high,
there is no low,

just levels of something
taller or below.

If you think going

to China is far,

what would you think about
going to a star?

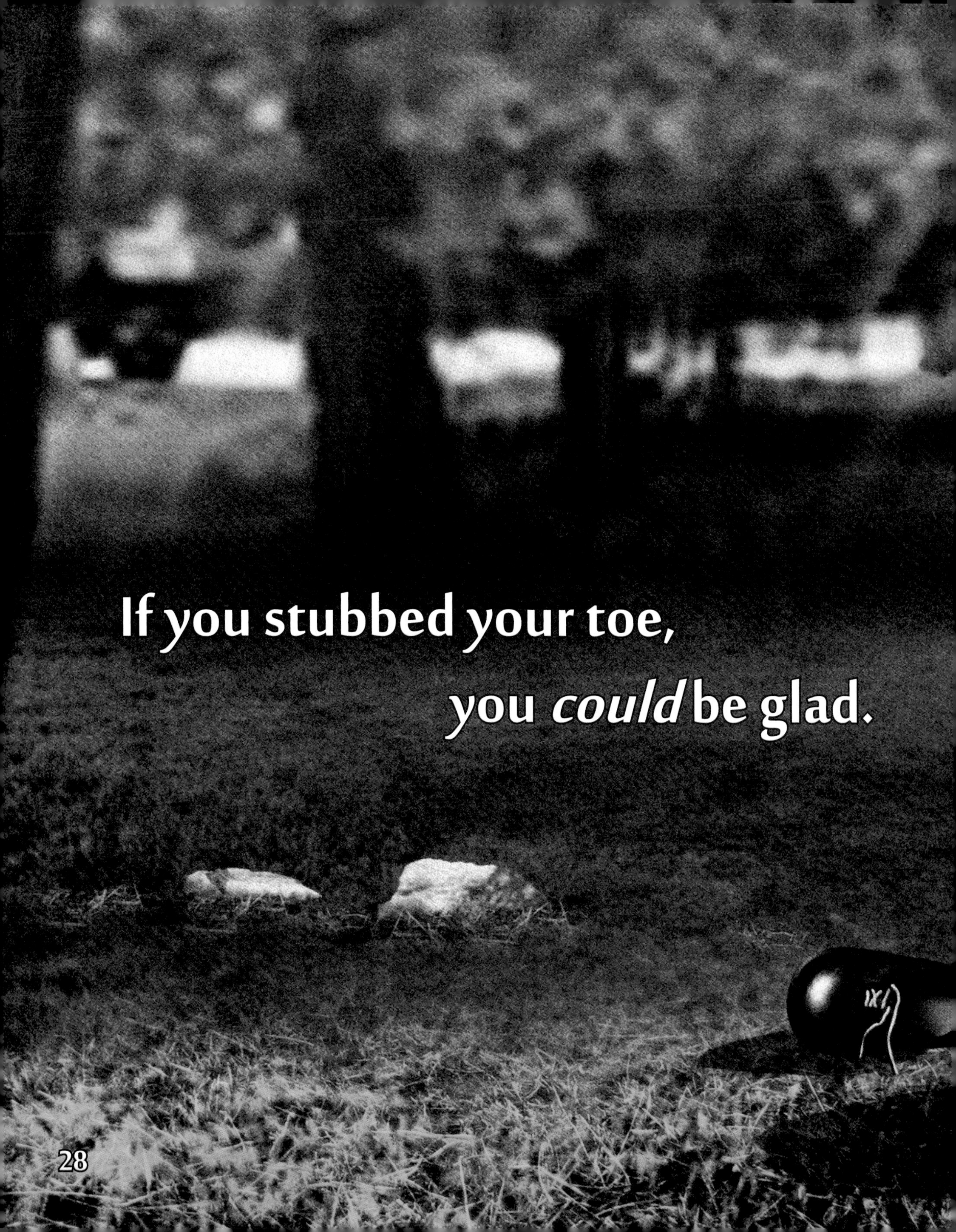

If you stubbed your toe,

you *could* be glad.

If your toe fell off,

THAT! would be really bad.

So, the next time you look at
something good, or bad,
or fast, or slow,

or anything you can see,

just think a thought about

RELATIVITY.

To my loving wife, Vianney, and our son, Oliver.
—Octavio Oliva

For kids who know that the world is not simply black and white.
—Michael Smith

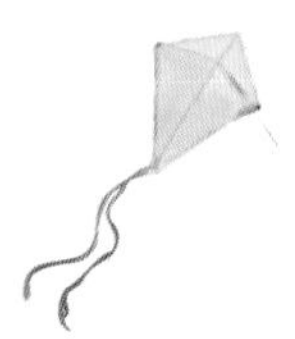

Published by East West Discovery Press
P.O. Box 3585, Manhattan Beach, CA 90266
Phone: 310-545-3730, Fax: 310-545-3731
Website: www.eastwestdiscovery.com

Written by Michael Smith
Illustrated by Octavio Oliva
Edited by Marcie Rouman
Design and production by Icy Smith and Jennifer Thomas

ISBN-13: 978-0-9799339-8-1 Hardcover
Library of Congress Control Number: 2010938862
First U.S. Edition 2011
Printed in China
Published in the United States of America